Self-Publish A Book:

Beginner Guide to Learn How to Self-Publish Your Own Book

Evan Miller

recorded copy and is only allowed with an expressed written consent from the Publisher. All additional rights reserved.

The information in the following pages is broadly considered to be a truthful and accurate account of facts and as such any inattention, use or misuse of the information in question by the reader will render any resulting actions solely under their purview. There are no scenarios in which the publisher or the original author of this work can be in any fashion deemed liable for any hardship or damages that may befall them after undertaking information described herein.

Additionally, the information in the following pages is intended only for informational purposes and should thus be thought of as universal. As befitting its nature, it is presented without assurance regarding its prolonged validity or interim quality. Trademarks that are mentioned are done without written consent and can in no way be considered an endorsement from the trademark holder.

Table of Contents

Introduction

Congratulations on downloading *Self-Publish A Book: Beginner's Guide to Learn How to Self-Publish Your Own Book* and thank you for doing so.

The following chapters will discuss what the process of self-publishing and how you can publish your very own book in a matter of days. Most people think that, to become a successful author, it is fundamental to go through publishers. However, this is not the case anymore, since Amazon and other sites allow writers to post their book for free. If, in addition, we put in a little bit of promotion, the results can be as good as using "official" publishers.

In this book, we will dive into the process of self-publishing your own book and how you can apply the same strategies we explain to offer your amazing writing skills to the world.

Please note that the same process can be applied for self-publishers that are outsourcing books and want to establish a business more than a reputation as good writers. The same strategies apply both for fiction and non-fiction topics, so do not worry.

There are plenty of books on this subject on the market, thanks again for choosing this one! Every effort was made to ensure it is full of as much useful information as possible, please enjoy!

Chapter 1: How to Choose the Right Title for the Book

The title can be chosen from the beginning. It can be likened to a hook that attaches the rest of the book, or as an inexhaustible source of energy. Or the title can be a light at the end of the tunnel.

In other cases, it remains for a long time as only a reminder; a synthetic label to synthesize a much more complex reality.

There is always time to find the definitive title. However, at a certain point, it is necessary to choose the title. You need to do it well because this is the real calling card of a book.

For example, how would we read James Joyce's Ulysses, if he had chosen a different title?
The title is an integral part of a book - and guessing it is a key ingredient of his fortune.

Especially if the author or publisher is a rookie. But how do you find the right title?

For Milan Kundera, "any book of mine could be called The Unbearable Lightness of Being" or "The Joke or Loving Amor." The titles are interchangeable and reflect the small number of themes that obsess, define and, unfortunately, limit him.

With great pragmatism, the publisher Alfred Knopf reproached Dashiell Hammett: "You should take care of yourself and worry a little more about your titles. When a person cannot pronounce the title or the name of the author, he becomes intimidated and no longer dares to enter the library to request that book. It happens more often than you may not think". You have to keep an eye on the reader, especially if you consider him a buyer.

In the search for the best solution, numerous titles have been changed during the course of work, by the authors or by the editors. So, we cannot read: "First impressions" by Jane Austen (Pride and Prejudice), The Sea Cook by Robert Louis Stevenson (Treasure Island), The Whale of Hermann Melville (Moby Dick), Judah: A Story of Christ by Joseph Sinkiewicz (Ben-Hur), The Last Man of Europe by George Orwell (1984), The Kingdom by the Sea by Vladimir Nabokov (Lolita), Before This Anger by Arthur Hailey (Roots), Birds and Woody's Bees Allen (All you wanted to know about sex (but dared not ask)). You see, all these titles were changed many times, but today they resemble the quintessence of literature.

A title of unquestionable effectiveness such as "Gone with the Wind" was preceded, while Margaret Mitchell wrote her masterpiece, from "Pansy" (as it was originally called the protagonist Scarlett O'Hara), from "Tote the Weary Load" (the verse of a song) and from "Tomorrow is another day (the unforgettable phrase of the unforgettable Scarlett)."

David Herbert Lawrence has changed his titles very often, with tormented but happy decisions: "Paul Morel" became "Sons and Lovers," "John Thomas and Lady Jane" became "Lady Chatterley's lover," "The Sisters" became "The Rainbow" and "The Marriage Ring" became "Women in Love."

Adolf Hitler also gave "Mein Kampf" another title: "Four And A Half Years Of Struggle Against Lies, Stupidity, And Cowardice." However, every book that has been successful had a great title that stands out.

There are essentially two main methods to select

the perfect title for the book. Let's take a look at them.

FIRST METHOD: THE HEMINGWAY METHOD

Ernst Hemingway inspired this initial method. He makes a list of titles after finishing the story or the novel - sometimes even a hundred. Then he started to cancel them, or delete them all and start over again.

SECOND METHOD: THE COPY AND PASTE METHOD

Take the bestseller rankings of the last few years. If you want, you can restrict your selection to the genre of your novel and its rankings. Copy the titles patiently and count the most frequently used words. Choose the terms that best fit your novel and combine them as best you can: you will get a title that points straight to the top of the standings.

If you want to give a more scientific approach to the procedure, you can use a corrective factor. This occurs by adding the sales index of the books in which it appears for each word in the titles in the ranking.

You will thus obtain a ranking of the bestseller words, which will certainly facilitate your task.

You can check with a quick survey in the library that many editors use this method to choose the titles of the novels they publish.

Furthermore, there are seven other different tips and tricks that can help you choose the right title for the book. Here is a list of strategies that can really make your book stand out from the title.

1. Look for your title in your book and let others look for it. A trusted reader could find hidden inside some sentences, the perfect title that you, would never have managed to identify.

2. Look for your title in the books you read.

3. Look for your title among the verses of poets. Often there are verses that when isolated, can become perfect titles. The first example that comes to mind is a recent book by Benedetta Tobagi whose title, "How I Beat Your heart," is the last verse of "Any Case," a poem by Wislawa Szymborska.

4. Always remember that it does not depend on the beauty of the title to determine if your manuscript will be published or not by a publishing company. In a manuscript, the title counts very little. Often the final titles are chosen by the editors, naturally with the agreement of the author. However, since we are talking about self-publishing, this is even a smaller problem.

5. There are no rules for the right title. If you walk around in the book-store, it may

seem like there are rules because most of the books you see are respecting them. This, however, is an illusion. If you returned two years later in that same bookshop you would find other rules, sometimes even opposed to those found in the previous visit. The rules are therefore very ephemeral, and the biggest mistake would be to choose the title with the hope of appending to a fashion and then maybe see their book go out in the book-store when that fashion has already passed and is considered old.

For the title, however, the general rule that has already been stated regarding the incipit is valid: it must not deceive the reader. Umberto Eco tells in the Postils, "The name of the rose": "My novel had another title, which was the Abbey of the crime. I discarded it because it fixes the reader's attention only on the police plot and could illicitly induce unfortunate buyers, hunting for stories all action, to throw themselves on a book that would have disappointed them."

6. Try not to think about the title until you have finished the novel and if you already have a headline does not make the mistake of caring too much.

7. And finally, remember that for every book there are many and different perfect titles.

Chapter 2: How to Protect Your Book from Being Copied

To protect the copyrights on a creation, there are no formal acts like registration of the work or a contract with the publisher. On the contrary, one becomes a father of the work at the very moment in which it is created. In addition, the right to paternity and economic exploitation is acquired, with the consequent possibility of interdicting, for the future, the third parties plagiarism and exploitation of a work.

The author must take care only of proving the anteriority of his own creation with respect to any subjects who claim to own rights over the work. Because it is obvious that, in the meantime, one can claim to be the only author of a work, since no one else can claim the same right for a creative process previously intervened. How to say: "The first who arrives, take everything!"

It is not worth claiming to be the first creators and acquire the copyright. If then, this circumstance cannot be demonstrated in a courtroom.

In this sense, it is essential to demonstrate a certain date in which we have become authors. This is done to prevent plagiarism.

To this end, the deposit of the work at the SIAE is the most classic and secure method for attributing authorship to the work and providing it with a certain date. But it is not the only one.

It is certainly not enough to insert the well-known symbol "©" of the copyright or the wording "all rights reserved," followed by a name and a date. These textual elements only indicate that we are the holders of the economic rights of the work, but they do not prove anything.

Many authors usually send a package with registered A / R addressed to themselves, containing the work to be protected. The delivery has the important task of taking care to keep it unconscious and sealed.

The postmark certifies the date of sending the registered letter, as placed on the parcel by a public official. This would guarantee the sending date. When this occurs, the work already existed.

The system, however, even if it is the most economical and easy to perform, is also the most insecure. Not infrequently, postal packages arrive at their destination under conditions that are not optimal, torn and in some cases even unglued. Furthermore, it is very easy to replace the contents of the package and, although tampered with, make it seem sealed. Moreover, the law assigns the test value to the postmark only when the wrapping forms a single body with the work sent. This occurs when the sheet of paper is folded on itself, and the address of the addressee is written and affixed to the postmark.

An alternative system can be to send the package

to any of the public bodies, which have the obligation to endorse, annotate and record what they receive by post. So often we send a registered letter with return receipt, containing your work, to the Presidency of the Republic. Once the correspondence has been opened, the institution will record in its register the date of receipt of the product (a cd, a score, a book, etc.).

Even this system, however, appears to be not very effective due to three reasons:

1. The slow response of the Administrations.
2. The ease of dispersion of documents within their archives and the impossibility of keeping them for an unlimited time.
3. The difficulty, in the absence of an exact identification of the product in the register, to identify the document with accuracy among the many received.

It is sometimes used to exploit the provisions of Law 106/2004, which requires the deposit of all works in the National Archives of the Editorial Production. But, beyond the failure to fulfill this formality does not correspond to any penalty. The obligation concerns only the works already published and, not those so to speak "homemade."

In any case, this fulfillment has a purely administrative and non-evidential value.

Other ways to prove the authorship of the work are the various forms of publication that document with certainty the date of public performance. These include newspapers, newspapers, magazines, television, and radio. Even a performance in public where the work was presented is appropriate, will be tested with a dignified record having a somehow certain date and/or with witnesses.

The testimonial test, however, is the weakest one.

Another great tool that can be used to protect the

copyrights of your book is Copyzero. It is a system to register the copyright of a work online. Personally, I have never used it, and I do not know anyone who has. However, it seems an economic method that would be interesting to test the effectiveness. It is a system that allows putting the digital signature on a file to be able to demonstrate the paternity on a certain date.

Furthermore, if you are thinking about publishing a paperback version of your book as well, you need to think about purchasing an ISBN. What is it? Let's dive into that!

The International Standard Book Number (ISBN) is a number that uniquely and permanently identifies a title or edition of a particular publisher's title internationally.

The current ISBN consists of a 13-digit string, divided into 5 sectors. Only the first and last sectors have a fixed number of digits (respectively 3 and 1). Whereas the other three central sectors the number of figures varies inversely proportionally. Sometimes the various sectors of the ISBN are separated from each other by a hyphen or by a space.

N.B. Human readable ISBN can be shown with hyphens or spaces

EAN prefix - are the first three digits of the ISBN, introduced starting in 2007. This indicates that you are in the presence of a book.

Linguistic group - is the identifier of the country or the linguistic area of the publisher. This can use 1 to 5 digits.

Publisher - is the identifier of the publishing

house or the publishing brand; can use from 2 to 7 digits.

Title - is the identifier of the book; can use from 1 to 6 digits.

Control character - is the last digit of the ISBN. In the "old" ISBN-10 codes, in addition to the numbers from 0 to 9, it was also used the Roman 10, i.e. the "X." This serves to verify that the code it has not been read or incorrectly transcribed. This can always happen, especially when using automated tools such as barcode readers.

The application of the ISBN code is essential to make the work traceable in the list of books on the market. To publish a book and make it possible to purchase it on online stores or at physical libraries, it is necessary to request the application of the ISBN code. Moreover, the attribution of the code implies a VAT tax of 4%, and not of 21% on the cost per copy in the case of printing.

Since 2015 even self-published authors (which

the ISBN agency calls "author publishing") may have a code for their books, whose structure is similar to that of the code for the publisher. The variance occurs only in the three figures of the world of the book (979 instead of 978), linguistic identification (12 instead of 88) and the prefix editor (which is 200).

To get an ISBN, if you're a self-published author, you can choose between two ways:

1. Purchase it on the Agency's website.
2. Obtain it for free by publishing through the self-publishing platforms that provide it (including Amazon KDP in the new paper-making beta function).

Let's see them both.

If you decide to buy the code from the site of the Agency, it will be yours and will identify you as a self-published author. Simply sign up and access the section dedicated to publishing.

The ISBN does have a standard cost, so before deciding whether to buy or not, make your considerations.

You can buy from 1 to 5 codes. Please note that it is logical that if you have more titles, editions or formats, it is better to buy more codes and save.

1 code: 80 euros + VAT

2 codes: 150 euros + VAT

3 codes: 220 euros + VAT

4 codes: 280 euros + VAT

5 codes: 340 euros + VAT

In addition to the code, the digits include the barcodes and the ISBN-A. That is operable, an additional service that "returns the user the information and services that the publisher has associated with the book."

If you are tight on budget or do not want to spend any money, you can rely on the ISBN platforms such as Amazon, CreateSpace or Streetlib offer for free. However, these codes do not identify you as the author. However, the platform essentially becomes your publishing house.

The same KDP warns that the e-books published in its platform do not need ISBN and that they will be assigned a code called ASIN. For paper copies, however, it is essential.

Since a paper without ISBN cannot be distributed, you will not be able to finish in bookstores. Often scammer publishers do not assign ISBNs to their books. If you realize that this is about to happen to you, run away!

Chapter 3: How to Publish a Book on Amazon and Lulu

Lulu

After countless refusals received by a publishing house, have you decided to try the self-publishing route and publish your first book on the Internet? Excellent choice, because by taking this route, you can make your work known to a potentially vast public, spending little or nothing.

Earnings? If you want to get those, perhaps it is better to proceed in small steps and begin by proposing to readers a book downloadable for free or, at reasonable prices.

The decision is then made! Cut out a few minutes of free time and find out how to publish a book on the Internet by researching the various services listed below. They are all extremely reliable and easy to use.

The first self-publishing platform that I recommend you try is Lulu. Here, you can publish your works online in the form of eBooks which are done at no cost. Printed books have a variety of affordable price packages.

After connecting to your home page, fill out the form at the top right. Sign up and publish for free by typing your name, email address and the password you want to use to access your user profile. Then click on the "Create an account button" to start the book publishing process.

On the page that opens, click on the "My Lulu" button and choose whether to create a paper book or an eBook using one of the two buttons in the panel of your user profile. I advise you to start with an eBook as they are easier to publish and distribute. They are also completely free for those who publish them.

At this point, depending on the choice you made in the previous step, you must type the title to be assigned to your eBook and your name or pen name. Then, choose the print quality of the paper book that you intend to publish. The cheapest books are with a soft cover and thermal binding and cost 3.80 euros / 100 pages. If you want to calculate the cost of multiple copies of a work printed wholesale click on the item titled, "Wholesale Price" and select the number of books to produce through the drop-down menu that appears below.

After choosing the type of book to create and having assigned a title to the latter, control the check-mark next to the entry to get a free ISBN from Lulu. This ensures that you can publish the work not only on Lulu but also on Amazon and other stores. Finally, click on Save and Continue twice in a row. Next comes the most important part!

Click on the "Choose File / Browse" button and select the file containing your book. You can use Microsoft Word DOC / DOCX documents, PDF files, eBooks in ePub and text in RTF or TXT format. I recommend, however, before proceeding to upload a file to make sure that it meets Lulu's requirements for distribution and is correctly formatted.

After choosing the file, click on Upload to upload it to Lulu and wait for the operation to finish. Be patient as it may take a few minutes. Then, click on the Save and Continue button, and wait for the site to process the work to fit the standard size of a book. Finally, click on "Save and continue" to design a cover for your publication.

After passing this important step, fill out the form that is proposed to you by selecting the category your book belongs, the license you intend to distribute it, and a short description in the appropriate text field. To conclude, click on Save and continue. Choose the distribution channels to which to assign the work (only Lulu or even Amazon, Kobo, iBooks etc.) and set the selling price of the product using the text field located above right.

Changing the price of the public sale of the work (which can also be 0 euros), next to the logo of each store you will be shown the number of your earnings and fees that are automatically withheld by Lulu and other stores for each work sold. Once you have chosen the price of your eBook/book, click on Revise the project to view a summary of the preferences you have set previously and confirm everything to start the publication.

Amazon

Are you an aspiring writer and would you like to sell your first works online? Then Amazon is the best resource available to you. If you want to distribute your books in electronic format, it is one of the best solutions you can find. It has a large audience and allows you to do everything in no time.

Following the guide I am about to propose, you can find out how to publish a book on Amazon in a totally free way. Also, your work will be for sale at the price you want within twenty-four hours. Try it and good luck with your career as a writer!

Before seeing in detail how to publish a book on Amazon, you have to do a couple of very important operations. First, if you have not done it yet, you have to register for Amazon Free. It takes only a few seconds.

Next, you must prepare your book for publication on Amazon complying with all the parameters required for its layout (index, chapters, cover, etc.). You can find all the information you need in the official Amazon guide to prepare books in electronic format. All the most common types of digital documents are supported, but it is recommended to use the HTML format or Word DOC / DOCX.

After signing up to the site and preparing your masterpiece for good, you can publish a book on Amazon by connecting to this Web page and clicking on the Login button located on the right. Then log in with your Amazon account information and complete your profile by clicking on the Update link at the top. You will need to fill in two forms: one with your personal information (name, address and telephone number) and one with your tax information. You must clarify if you are a private individual or a company if you are a US citizen and answer other questions that you will allow you to validate your identity and proceed with the publication of the book.

After having provided Amazon with all the requested data, go back to the initial page of the Direct publishing service and click on the button "Add a New Title" to start publishing your eBook. Then fill out the form that is proposed to you with all the information related to your work, such as title, description, cover, gender, the price of sale to the public, etc. Then, click on the Save and Continue button to complete the book publishing process.

As for the economic side of the issue, the publication of books on Amazon is free and you can collect royalties for a total of 70% on the sales of the work if you choose a price between 2.60 and 9.70 euros or 35% if prices between 0.86 and 173.91 euros are chosen (in all markets). You can also join the KDP Select program that allows you to expand the availability of the book to the international versions of Amazon and to get some money even from the loan of the work. This occurs while maintaining an exclusivity on the digital dissemination of the book. Find all the details on the Amazon page dedicated to the royalty's management system for authors.

CreateSpace

To publish a book on CreateSpace, which is a company owned by Amazon that allows authors and publishers to publish the paperback version of their books, you need only two things: the PDF of your book and the PDF of the cover. Ye can proceed without them, just to take a look, but you cannot complete the publication procedure.

For clarity, here is an example of the characteristics of the book we want to publish. (The following formats are also accepted: .doc, .docx, .rtf).

Example:
Book in 6" x 9" format (15.24 cm x 22.86 cm) consisting of 120 pages in black and white printed on white paper.

We access our profile and go to the Dashboard; the control panel from where we can manage all our publications.

Step by step process to publish on CreateSpace

Click on [Add New Title], and the Title Information window will appear.

In this window we do not have to enter all the information; only some of them are mandatory such as:

1. Book's title.
2. The subtitle of the book.
3. Main author (only the first and last name will suffice)
4. If the author is more than one or you need to insert curators, translators and other figures who have collaborated in the creation of the book, you can enter them here by choosing the most appropriate item (Edited by, Authored by, Translated by, etc.).

5. Select if the publication is part of a series.

6. Here we can enter the title of the series (Series Title) and the relative number (Volume). Example. Title: Roman cuisine.

7. The edition number is useful if the new publication is a reissue of a previous one.

8. Language in which the text is written.

9. The publication date can be left blank and will be automatically added when we complete all the registration phases of our book.

Once the required information is completed, we save and continue.

Getting an ISBN through CreateSpace
Remember when I told you the importance of having an ISBN? To get in on Createspace, you have two options:

1. Let you assign an ISBN from CreateSpace for FREE; (recommended)

2. Provide CreateSpace with our code

previously purchased through an ISBN agency.

After having completed this information, you will be asked to send your book for validation. It will take only 24 hours before you will be able to get a preview of what the customer will get, once the order has been placed. You can either get a paperback version, for a very low price, or a digital version.

Chapter 4: Other Publishing Platforms and Consideration Points

Once you have written and corrected your novel, you are finally ready to publish it.

You now have to choose the self-publishing platform that best suits your needs.

What are these needs? It's simple: earnings, distribution, costs.

Your book is a product, and as such, it should be sold. Do not throw yourself into business if you do not know who or what you have before you.

Publishing without criteria will not lead you to anything. Unfortunately, you will pay a lot of money without any income.

In this chapter, we will discuss how to choose the right self-publishing platform. Once you have finished reading, you will know which channel is best suited to your needs.

Premise: your needs

As I told you before, your main needs are three:

- Earnings.
- Distribution.
- Costs.

It's imperative to remember these three details:

➢ You cannot choose a self-publishing platform if you do not know the number of royalties you will get.

➢ You cannot choose a self-publishing platform if you do not know where, or how your book will be distributed.

➢ You cannot choose a self-publishing platform if you do not know what the initial costs are.

Not all self-publishing platforms are the same. Some act like real publishers and also offer editorial and promotional services. Others are simple print-on-demand (POD). Depending on what you want for your book, you can choose between one or the other platform.

Let's discuss these needs one by one.

Earnings

We often hear the saying that everyone is writing for the glory, for a hobby, or for a passion. Is that really the case? In addition, is it so absurd to say that one writes to make money? After all, writing is a job. How many of us spend hours bending over a sheet of paper or on the keyboard? Is this not considered work?

So do not be ashamed if making a solid income is an influential part of your needs.

When looking for the right self-publishing

platform, you first need to consider what percentage of royalty you will receive on each copy sold.

This is a very important point because often some self-publishing or print on demand platforms offer different gains. Often, this can make a significant difference.

In a previous chapter on Kindle Direct Publishing, you saw how Amazon offers two percentages of royalties depending on the price of the book: 35% and 70%.

The platform, You Can Print, gives you 20% of the cover price for each hard copy sold in bookstores and online stores. This rises to 30% for sales on the You Can Print store. As for the e-book, you will receive 50% for sales on online stores excluding You Can Print. Moreover, you are entitled to 70% of sales on You Can Print.

With Streetlib, the profit percentage is 60% for each copy sold.

Kobo has a similar mechanism to Amazon: the percentage is 45% for a price ranging from 0 to 1.98 euros, and 70% from 1.99 euros up.

Distribution

This aspect is only useful if you intend to publish the paper format of your book.

Many self-publishing platforms, in fact, also give you the opportunity to distribute your book in physical book-stores, such as Mondadori. It is very interesting since you will have the opportunity to "physically" reach more readers.

You Can Print gives you the chance to see your book distributed in over 4,500 book-stores. However, You Can Print informs you that your book will not be distributed immediately, but only ordered. This means that every bookseller can decide whether or not to order a book.

Even with Streetlib, you can sell your book "physically" in a book-store.

Other platforms, however, reserve this service for foreign customers only, as in the case of Lulu.

You can also decide to print the hard copy of your book and sell it through online stores such as Amazon and its Createspace service. It's still an opportunity because not everyone reads digital.

Costs

Many believe that self-publishing is free of cost. It is a myth that should be debunked. Self-publishing has its costs, and one of these represents the publication phase.

When you're looking for the right self-publishing platform, indicate how much you have to spend first. This planning will help to alleviate stress and assist with the process.

If considering e-books, the only cost you have is the assignment of an ISBN, which you can buy on the agency's website.

During the publication, Amazon informs us that it is not necessary to have an ISBN since it will assign a unique code for each e-book (ASIN). However, it is always good, if possible, to assign an ISBN to your book.

The publishing houses typically give an ISBN for each version of the book: paper and digital. Even some change ISBN for each sales platform (Kobo, Amazon).

As for paper, numerous print-on-demand platforms give you the opportunity to have a cost estimate for a total of printed copies. For example, if you want to print 50 copies of a 200-page book with You Can Print, they will provide an estimate.

After selecting among some available options, the total cost is 279.47 euros. This includes shipping and assignment of the ISBN.

Other needs?

Consider a few intricate details that could influence your decision.

For example, what are the rights of your book? Do they remain to you, as in the case of the Kindle Unlimited service? Or, are you bound to stay only on the Kindle Direct Publishing platform?

Does the platform also provide additional services such as graphics, layout, and editing? If you need them, you can consider the platforms that make them available, even if there are not many.

And finally: what constraint do I have with the platform? Can I withdraw the book when I want, or

should I wait a significant amount of time?

Whatever your needs, you must carefully evaluate them one by one before choosing the self-publishing platform. Fortunately, no choice is final, and in most cases, you can try a few of them, before sticking with one.

Chapter 5: How to Gather Reviews and Promote Your Book

Getting good reviews on Amazon is challenging. It is not easy to satisfy a customer to the point that you reward yourself with the time necessary to write good feedback. In this chapter, we'll show you how to get better feedback using transactional emails.

What are Amazon reviews based on?

Customer expertise is increasing as they know all about the product before buying it. Before deciding for your online store, they have already collected information and compared your product with that of competitors, until something in your offer does not convince them to choose you. One of these elements is your reviews. From the moment they know everything about the product you are selling (price, characteristics, competitors, etc.), the purchase decision is linked to the experience that the user thinks he can have with your online store. By reading the reviews of other customers, a user can understand how good your book is.

Both decisions and reviews are changing from product-centric to experience-centric. Users do not share information about the product, which can be easily found anywhere. Rather, they determine the shopping experience with your online store: both delivery times and, above all, quality of communication and clarity of information.

The customer wants to feel safe with you, always informed, kind and that you are a reliable seller.

You can easily get all this by using transactional emails.

What are transactional emails?

Transactional e-mails are communications with the user that are sent according to a specific user action. These are the e-mails that record the highest opening rate as they contain important information for the user. The simplest example is the e-mail that the user receives as confirmation of a completed purchase. Please, remember that if you are working with a third party platform, like Amazon, this process is made by the publishing platform on your behalf. Less work for you!

Why are they important during the user's purchasing process?

In most cases, we are talking about e-mails. Since they act as a confirmation that the purchase process has developed in the right way and that everything has worked properly, it is always a pleasure to get them.

The user is so used to receiving them when shopping online that the non-receipt of them is perceived as a sign of something wrong, leaving the user disappointed and lowering the degree of trust towards the seller.

Transactional e-mails are an essential element for customers to keep track of their orders, receive useful information on the status of the shipment and get dedicated discounts in relation to their favorite products.

Good communication + shopping experience = 5-star reviews on Amazon!

We think there are some "must-have" transactional emails for your book. As we said, good communication is the main way to have satisfied customers. Send an email to confirm the purchase, one to confirm the shipment, updates on the status of the shipment (track & trace emails), one to request a review when the customer is at maximum satisfaction.

The moment when the customer receives his order is perfect to send an email request for feedback. This message allows you to write the customer a friendly request for a review of the experience with your store. Buyers often leave no reviews and sellers do not require them. Reviews on Amazon and other marketplaces are essential to gaining valuable impressions on how to improve the experience you offer. In addition, customers who do not leave reviews on Amazon can be an obstacle to gaining reputation.

Contact your customer with a friendly email when he is satisfied and excited. This can occur when initially received the order - leaving a link for review, allows you to receive more reviews with a stronger emotional content.

One vital question, however, might be, "how long does it take me to set up all this stuff?"

As often happens, the correct question is how much money you waste if you do not implement the actions. If the transactional e-mails contain valuable information that the customer wants to know and receive, what about the non-delivery of them?

When the buyer cannot find the information he is looking for, he starts the search by beginning to contact the company through various tools such as telephone, Facebook page, direct e-mail, etc. In short, not implementing these communications generates a sense of disservice and loss for the customer. This could even result in an exponential increase in time dedicated to customer care.

Activating a strategy to send good communications involves better management, time savings and improvements in the performance of your self publishing business. All this for an investment of minimum time, if you use a tool to automate the sending of transactional emails such as those described below.

What are the most used tools to manage these communications?

Generally, transactional e-mails, when managed, are sent through different tools, not all of them performing and customizable: CRM, courier web services, marketplace infrastructure.

As it is easy to understand, this fragmented management and delegation to different tools and platforms can cause inefficiencies and errors in the information provided and in terms of updating them. For example, no CRM is currently able to offer the track & trace, nor to coordinate the actions of the courier with the transactional emails that are sent to the customer.

There is software able to guarantee centralization in the management of information to make the management of transactional e-mails more efficient through a single control panel.

A direct approach on how to get reviews on Amazon

In recent weeks we have witnessed the scandal of false reviews, of authors who have paid to get them or that they have signed under a false name. Whatever your opinion, these episodes only confirm how critical reviews are in pushing sales of a book.

Everyone wants to get good reviews, but the wait to be able to build an audience, which naturally expresses their consent, can be really long.

One way to get authoritative and quality reviews are to submit your book to the top Amazon customers for a review.

Why should an author point right to them?

1. These users prove to be strong readers, who read more books a week and therefore are likely to receive an immediate response.

2. They know how to make useful and discreet reviews. In fact, being able to fit in the ranking of the TOP CUSTOMERS of the most important e-commerce site in the world, is not just a question of numbers, how many reviews on the products you can publish, in fact, there are users who will have produced more than 7000 reviews, but at the moment in first place there is a user who wrote only 671.

As always, Amazon uses a complex algorithm to organize its rankings, and in this case, the positions of reviewers are determined by the percentage of usefulness and appreciation expressed by the others community users. Now, since the position is as much coveted as it is difficult to reach, you can be sure that the most active commentators put so much attention and energy into their reviews. Which is good news, because that's what makes them the best and most convincing.

3. They are often authors of literary blogs and have a good following on social networks to benefit from in terms of media exposure.

4. Approval by one of these users will also give prominence to your Amazon page. In fact, as confirmed by a recent survey on self-publishing done by Taleist, authors who get popular reviews receive on Amazon 25% more comments and 32% more revenues than average.

However, there are also negative aspects, and it is right to mention them:

- Doing this research and doing it well takes time and energy. Some users will explicitly say they do not want to be targeted. But this is part of the game.

Furthermore, they could be very critical and tough. It is important, when you do your research, to aim exactly at those who might be interested in your book.

How to get reviews on Amazon

1. Go to http://www.amazon.com/review/top-reviewers.

2. Click on the names that inspire you (make sure that these are book reviewers and not other products sold on Amazon).

3. Check which books they reviewed in the past.

4. Look for relevant information about their interests and hobbies.

5. Make sure that public contact information appears in the personal profile.

6. Send them a short excerpt of the book explaining.

- Why they could be passionate about your book

- How they can receive free copies

- Always thank them, no matter the response. They might say "No" the first time, but eventually, you will get their attention. Do not worry.

Do not forget that they are busy people and probably receive hundreds of such requests. So, make sure that the extract sent is short and pleasant to be read.

7. Aim to contact some users 3 or 4 times higher than the number of reviews you expect to receive, as some users will not respond at all.

8. Stand by and remain patient.

The journey to get high-quality reviews for your book can be long. It takes time and effort, but the reward will be great.

How to promote your book on Facebook

The extreme diffusion of Facebook along with its ease of use have pushed over the years more and more users to crowd on the social network of Zuckerberg to publish content daily.

A few years ago to gain visibility into a subject, only a few publications were enough in addition to positive reviews. Now, things on Facebook seem significantly changed and decidedly more complicated. What previously could have seemed like a simple game for kids has now become a real puzzle for experienced communication professionals made up of rules and best practices.

So if the goal is to have visibility on Facebook, then you must also have a strategy and understand the tricks of Facebook, especially if you want to promote your book.

So before launching into the barren sharing of supposedly catchy content, you need to stop and think about what needs to be done, perhaps by filling out a small list for points: what, how, when and where to promote on Facebook.

What to promote

On Facebook, to gain visibility, it is always necessary to create content that is new and original that can some way interest other users. The real problem is that quality content is very often unobtainable. Therefore it is clear that the first thing to do is to identify the object of communication and all the possible connections with it. Wanting to take a practical example, let's imagine we want to promote a book on Facebook.

It is necessary to understand the contents to be discarded and which ones are useful. The last category certainly includes the title of the book, the cover, a brief description, the introduction, information on the author and the publishing house.

Finally, a synopsis of no less than 500 words, subsequently divided into several parts and inserted into publications or comments or private messages. Very useful are also links to any reviews on the web or other images related to the book itself. If you decide to promote a comic book on Facebook, it might be interesting to have some pictures of the sketches of the drawings to show the most curious users how to create a character and its history. Or again, it could be a good idea to have the interviews, video links to the author or the dates of the book presentations. In addition, some significant passages that could intrigue Facebook users without revealing the crucial nodes of the story.

Therefore, in this phase, it is useful to collect as much material as possible. This is not limited to the creation of graphic banners for the possible promotion of the book while trying to satisfy all the possible curiosity of the users. All the while, maintaining the contents published on Facebook as always fresh, original and quality.

How to promote

On Facebook, the main tool for promoting content is represented by the post.

This can be a simple text, an image (or an album), a link, a video, etc. Regardless of the nature of the content, they post on Facebook must have certain characteristics to aim to get the greatest possible visibility within the social network of Zuckerberg.

Statistics in hand, in fact, it has occurred that on Facebook the post with the greatest chance of being read is the one that presents within it some text (between 100 and 119 characters including spaces) accompanied by an image or a link or from a video. In the text, it is obviously necessary to insert the appropriate keywords. That is exactly those specific keywords for which you believe you want to be "found" by other Facebook users. These keywords must be organized not in the form of a sterile list, but in such a way that the text of the post is clear, captivating, able to intrigue and therefore generate debate among the users reached by the news. This aspect is too often overlooked and left to chance by most of those who promote a topic on the social network of Mark Zuckerberg.

Although on Facebook the debate through comments (the so-called "engagement") of a post certainly represents a powerful tool for promotion, not many self-publishers take it into account. Thanks to the comments of the post it is possible on the one hand to improve and refine the message object of the communication on Facebook, on the other hand, to fully understand the preferences of the other users. Creating invariably further ideas for the promotion and consequently attracting new traffic of users interested in the topic.

When to promote

Once understood "what" and "how" to promote nothing remains but to understand the "when."

In fact, as for other social networks, even for Facebook it is possible to identify "best moments" within which it is more convenient to publish or comment on a post. Therefore data at hand (Source BlitzLocal) it turns out that for the social network of Mark Zuckerberg the most convenient time slots for sharing content are substantially two:

a) Between six and eight in the morning;

b) Between two and five o'clock in the afternoon from monday to friday.

Obviously, these time periods must be treated as simple general indications susceptible to more or less sensitive variations depending on the topic that you want to promote on Facebook. In fact, it is natural to think that users interested for example in a cookbook can have different habits than those who are passionate about comics or thrillers.

Here is a list of other ways you can use to promote your book

1. Take surveys

Test your demographics of your audience

and their online preferences. In this way, you can understand where to find your potential readers and which type of communication they respond to best. You can propose surveys to those already following you and to readers of authors of your own genre.

2. Interview readers

Try to understand how readers choose books to buy and read, where they find them, how they select them. Ask direct questions to get precise answers.

3. Create your type reader

Write a short paragraph describing exactly your type reader, or any type of reader you wish to reach. Whenever you want to create an advertisement or choose a cover for your new book, review what you've written to remember exactly the characteristics of your audience.

4. Create a list of keywords

Extend a list of keywords that your readers can use to search for books online. To help you can use tools like Google Trends or the Google Adwords Keyword Planner.

5. Create your site

Your site must become the hub of all your online activities, from creating a blog to the direct sale of your books, to the collection of email addresses to which you can send your newsletter. To create a site with ease you can use platforms such as WordPress, Squarespace or Wix com services.

6. Create a Blog on your site

Give your readers a glimpse of your writer's habits by posting one or two posts a month on your Blog. Readers like "behind the scenes," like to know the personality of an author and his writing process. Everything you post on the Blog can become the content of your newsletter that you send to your subscribers. This is called content recycling and works amazingly well for self-publishers.

7. Sell your books on your site

Create a page on your site where you present each one of your books, with the cover, a brief description, and links to all online book-stores where clients can buy them.

8. Customize the home page of your site

Every time you publish a new book, customize the home page of your site with special banners so that anyone entering the site has immediately before your eyes your last job. If you can, in the description of the book, instead of the back cover text, enter positive comments and feedback that you have received.

9. Build your own Mailing List

Insert a form on your website to collect the addresses of visitors to build your own Mailing List. This allows you to keep in touch with your readers.

10. Offer something in return to the email address

To entice readers to leave their email address, offer something in return, such as a story, or the first chapters of your new book, or a video, etc. With an autoresponder system, as soon as a reader enters his email, he immediately receives your gift in his mailbox. It is easy to set up works like magic!

11. Customize your Author Profile

Make sure your biographical notes or Author Page are always up-to-date, so readers can learn more about you and your books.

12. Open all your Social accounts with the same name

Make sure to always open your Social accounts with the same name, so that those looking for you can always find you. Even if you do not intend to use a social network actively, register the name so that no one else can then open an account on that Social with your same name.

13. Create your signature for emails

Create a personalized signature for your emails, so that anyone who receives an email from you can with a simple click visit your site or your Author Page on Amazon. In the same way insert the link to your Site also in your Social profiles, so that everything is connected.

14. Create a Vlog

Make simple videos and upload them to YouTube, creating a Vlog, ie a Video Blog. In these videos, you can answer readers' questions, interview other authors of your own genre, offer viewers your reading tips, read short excerpts from your books, etc. Each video, then, can be inserted into an article that you publish on your Blog. Try making a few short videos to see if you like this tool, before worrying about making high-quality videos.

15. Work with a professional graphic designer

A quality cover can have a big impact on

the sales of your book. For this reason, it is better to avoid the do-it-yourself and entrust the work to a professional graphic designer.

16. Try different covers

Ask the designer to make some variations of your cover and then submit them to public opinion. To compare two covers, one against the other, and decide which one you like best, you can use online tools like PickFu, UsabilityHub, or PlayBuzz.

17. Use the same graphics for books in series

If you have written books in series (a trilogy, for example) use the same graphics for the cover of each book in the series. Uniform graphics, the same character and the same position for the title help readers to recognize that they are linked to books and therefore to consider to buy also the following ones.

18. Republish a book with a new cover

Redesigning the cover of a book can be a great way to reinvigorate sales because it allows you to republish and re-launch it, keeping up with the changes in the public's taste.

19. Enter a short review of the book in the cover

If you've received a positive review from an authoritative source, consider adding a sentence taken from this review on your cover. Make it short, so readers will read it with a glance, and it will not be too intrusive in the cover art.

20. Make a preview of your book available

On Amazon, for example, readers can read an excerpt of your book before buying it by clicking on "Read the excerpt." This gives readers the opportunity to discover your style and, why not, to be interested in your story just enough to want to buy the book. It is a great way to attract new customers.

Chapter 6: 15 Things to Know About Self-Publishing

Self-publishing is within everyone's reach, but this does not mean that everyone knows how to do it the right way. A good text, of course, is the basic ingredient of success, but as in all things, there are few but fundamental rules to make headway in the world of DIY publishing.

1. You do not have to be a professional copy editor to know how to do it

No special degrees or masters are required: self-publishing a book is simple. Even easier it is done in e-books. Choose a format and prepare the manuscript in Word following those dimensions. Then create a cover in Photoshop and upload it to a self-publishing platform. Within a week or two, here you are with your first book in your hands, and the adventure begins.

2. Paper is nice but digital is better

Even if self-publishing attracts many because of the idea of having a paper book in your hands, never underestimate the potential of the digital format!

It is much easier to produce an e-book format book, especially for the formatting and design of the cover. And the cost can be much lower than paper, making the first sales easier!

3. Do not underestimate the quality!

Some services allow excellent quality prints or offer great tools for creating ebooks. Taking advantage of them also means presenting yourself with a reasoned design and a valid cover, not with a patched graphics project!

4. The truth is that competition can be very hard

The great thing about self-publishing is that anyone can do it. However, the problem with self-publishing is over saturation. You will find yourself among hundreds, thousands of authors, not all of high quality. It's up to you to challenge yourself to emerge in the indie market for books. But many examples show that a good product and a good word of mouth can emerge. Do you know that "50 Shades of Gray" was born as a self-published book?

5. Ability is something, but you need a little bit of luck and a lot of perseverance

If your book is mediocre, do not expect anything. But even if it is a masterpiece, there is a good chance that it will accumulate dust on the virtual shelves of online book-stores.

In other words: quality does not guarantee success, but it is an essential requirement. Make sure to take back the initial investment and count in luck. But above all, if you believe in your work, do not resign when you see the first difficulties.

6. Essays or romance

Some define this point as the mantra of self-publishing. Non-fiction books with a well-defined topic are great, especially if they have a defined target. For fiction, the topics do not all go the same way. And guess what? You need to learn to deal with this issue and make the most out of each one of your books.

7. The title is extremely important

"The thing," "The enchanted garden," "The strange case of Mr. Fog," "Everything you want to know about the shoe market in China," "Abandonment." Returning to the concept that your book, good or bad, it will end in a big sea of titles, it is easy to understand why it will be essential to have a powerful and functional title! Another point not to be underestimated, the book should be easily traceable through Google or the search engines of online stores. So it is good to do some indexation test before choosing the final title.

8. Do you really believe it? You could also ask for professional support (but look at the bill!)

If the largest publishers use a whole range of professional figures, there will be a reason. Copy editor, to verify the correct functioning of the text; marketing specialists to support their dissemination; Do you really believe in your book? You could think of involving somebody like that. But keep an eye on the fact that it is really worth it and that the investment is commensurate with the objective.

9. Do not neglect marketing

Even if you do not go to a specialist, do not believe you can go ahead without taking care of marketing. First of all, the choice of price is certainly not a change to be made so quickly, as if it was secondary. And remember that there will be no blogger who will come to review you spontaneously. Unless you find a way to convince him!

10. Self-publishing is a real physical sport

The biggest mistake you can make when publishing with self-publishing? To think that once the online title is put it is over and the sales are by themselves. The real secret of success is to have a well-defined promotion plan in mind, even before the publication, and to be ready to stand up in the jungle of the web! In fact, unlike a lot of publishers think, the real work begins once you have hit the "publish" button. It is at this point that the game starts. If you want to get a lot of money for your words, you cannot avoid taking the time to market your book properly. We have already discussed some of the main strategies, but keep in mind that the world is always changing and that you need to adapt, to succeed. Perseverance and a good attitude are two of the main ingredients to take your publishing business to the next level: do not give up.

Here are 5 mistakes that most beginners make when it comes to self-publishing.

1. Wait to send it until you feel it perfect

So it will not happen. Never. You will finish the last, very last revision, you will go to sleep joyful, convinced of having produced the Great Modern Novel, you will force to put it aside for a while to make a fresh reread with a fresh eye " just as a precaution "; after a week you will pick it up again and you will find dozens of things to change. Per page. And all this will be repeated N times. At some point, you have to take courage and throw your manuscript into the big world out there as it is. First step: proofreaders.

2. Skip proofreaders

Sometimes you have the balls to make your book read to an unknown publisher but not to someone who could really tell us what he thinks. The problem is that then, when the publisher's judgment arrives, if you are not prepared to risk crashing like a birch under a lightning bolt, and regret that no one has warned you before.

Choose the right people to submit your book to, perhaps write in turn, because no aspiring writer can resist the temptation to find the flaws in the work of a competitor.

3. Try multiple times with all publishers

Publishers, just like women, have their own character, their tastes, their visions of life. If you want to have a satisfying relationship, it is difficult to get in a room and try all the same strategy. Find those closest to your taste and presented by leveraging these affinities. You will be more considered, and you will save yourself a couple of stressful days. And, if you do not feel able, there are agents for this.

4. Neglect the cover letter

Once I received an editorial proposal accompanied by a note that only said: "Trust me: they are to be published." Many other times, I asked aspiring authors to introduce me their book and the answer was: "Well ... difficult to sum up like that ... It's a very special book ..." Be humble, come to meet the evaluator. To convince us, readers, to buy a book, the publisher slams down to write a back cover with which we can get an idea. Why should we demand that a publisher, to whom tsunami of manuscripts arrive per month, read our own from the beginning to the end only because we have assured him that it is "very particular" and "to be published"? If you can not present your book, maybe your book does not have such a strong identity.

5.   Refuse to be retouched

Then a publisher takes your manuscript and tells you that there is still some work to do. The idea is good, the characters too, but there are a couple of weak scenes, and the ending is disappointing. At this point you have two possibilities:

1) Decide that in publishing house are a bunch of incompetent bankrupt who put

on your novel perfectly conceived because it is known that those who can not criticize the work of others, or;

2) Think that in publishing house know their work and they are on your own side, since they have an interest in putting on the market a good book that will also bring their brand. If you have caught a publisher that you actually estimate, as mentioned above, the 2 is easier.

Conclusion

Thank you for making it through to the end of *Self-Publish A Book: Beginner's Guide to Learn How to Self-Publish Your Own Book*, let's hope it was informative and able to provide you with all of the tools you need to achieve your goals whatever they may be.

The next step is to start applying what you have learned during the course of this book and get started right away. Our suggestion is to make sure you follow the steps we laid out for you as close as possible because those are the right strategies that have allowed other people to become successful publishers. At this stage, you should have understood what it takes to become a self-published author: now it is your time to make a move and establish yourself in the writing community.

If you want to have more information about How to Self Publish a book, How to Write your Own

Book or How To Outline a Book check out my
Amazon Author page where you will find all my
guide to help you write and publish your own
book.

Finally, if you found this book useful in any way,
a review on Amazon is always appreciated!